ULTIMATE STICKER COLLECTION

How to use this book

Read the captions, then find the sticker that best fits the space.
(Hint: check the sticker label for clues!)

•

Don't forget that your stickers
can be stuck down and peeled off again.

•

There are lots of fantastic extra stickers
for creating your own scenes, too!

LONDON, NEW YORK, MELBOURNE,
MUNICH, and DELHI

Written by Shari Last
Edited by Ruth Amos and Shari Last
Designed by Toby Truphet and Richard Horsford

First published in the United States in 2014 by
DK Publishing
345 Hudson Street,
New York, New York 10014

10 9 8 7 6 5 4 3 2 1
001—196540—Mar/14

Published in Great Britain by Dorling Kindersley Limited.

A catalog record for this book is available
from the Library of Congress.

ISBN: 978-1-4654-1669-8

Color reproduction by Alta Image, UK
Printed and bound by L-Rex Printing Co., Ltd., China

Discover more at
www.dk.com
www.disney.com

FRIGHTENING FRIENDS

BOO! At the Monsters University School of Scaring, being scary is everything. Some students at this famous school are more frightening than others—and some are just too nice to be scary. Freshmen Sulley and Mike join forces and try to scare their way to the top of the class.

Sulley
Sulley is from a famous scaring family. He thinks it is easy to be scary—but he has a lot to learn!

Randy
Randy used to be friends with Mike, but now he and his new friends enjoy pranking Mike and Sulley.

Mike's Bike
Mike likes to ride his bike around campus and is great at pulling off high speed jumps!

School of Scaring
Monsters learn their skills at the School of Scaring, but most of their practice takes place out of the classroom.

Unlikely Friends
Sulley and Mike didn't get along at first, but they quickly realize they make a great scaring team!

Squishy
Squishy is so quiet, some people don't even notice he's there. This makes it easy for him to sneak up and shock people!

Art
Crazy monster Art scares everyone, just by being himself!

MIKE
Mike dreams of being a scarer when he grows up. He is so excited to study at the School of Scaring.

Backpack
Monsters University students are proud of their school. They wear lots of MU pins on their backpacks.

CAMPUS PRANKS

It's Fear-It week! Mike, Sulley, and their fellow students want to prove that Monsters University is the scariest school of all. But students from rival school Fear Tech are going to put up a fierce fight! To practice their scaring skills, everyone starts playing pranks on their fellow students.

Living in Fear
Fear-It Week puts all students on guard. Pranks are fun—but not when they are played on you! Sulley checks for any sign of a prank.

RELAXING
When he's not planning pranks, Sulley enjoys the beautiful campus.

Toilet Paper Launcher
Mike and Sulley love this gadget. They take aim, pull the trigger—and laugh as their target gets toilet papered!

Give 'Em a Hand
Beware as you walk past this advertising column. A giant hand is waiting inside to whack you!

No Place is Safe
Walking around campus can be risky. Watch out for pranks that are hidden in plain sight!

Go Fish Launcher
This looks like an everyday vending machine, but if you want a tasty snack, look elsewhere...

Phone It In Launcher
Steer clear of this phone booth. Instead of connecting calls, it connects a punch—to your face. Ouch!

Practice Makes Perfect
Sulley wants to be a top scarer, so he practices whenever he can. Look out, fellow students!

Fear Tech Monsters
Blocky and Crabby are Fear Tech students. They are planning to prank Mike, Sulley, and their friends.

Scare Team
Mike and Sulley spend lots of time discussing pranks, when they should be studying!

PIRATES AND PALS

Famous sailor of the seven seas, Jack Sparrow is the best pirate captain in the Caribbean. The oceans are under threat from the terrifying monster, the Kraken. Jack is on the hunt for the Kraken's Bane—the only weapon that can defeat the Kraken.

Captain Jack Sparrow
Jack Sparrow is a daring pirate and expert swordsman. He always has a trick up his sleeve.

CAPTAIN JACK
Jack has sailed all over the Caribbean. He thinks the seas should be free for everyone.

Davy Jones
Davy Jones is a sea monster who wants to rule the seven seas. His monster, the Kraken, terrifies all pirates.

Cursed Crew
Maccus, Turtle, Clam, and Driftwood are the cursed crew of Davy Jones's scary pirate ship.

Black Ship

Jack is fiercely proud of his beautiful pirate ship. The Black Ship is known as the fastest ship in the Caribbean.

Hector Barbossa

Hector Barbossa once betrayed Jack Sparrow and took control of his Black Ship. Now he joins Jack on his hunt for the Kraken's Bane.

Gibbs

Joshamee Gibbs is one of Jack's most loyal crew. When Joshamee is captured, Jack sets out to rescue him.

Treasure Hunt

Jack Sparrow is close to finding a piece of the Kraken's Bane. But hammerhead villain Maccus wants it for himself.

Tia Dalma

Tia Dalma is an ancient magician. She helps guide Jack and his crew as they race to find the Kraken's Bane.

Buccaneer Bay

Jack is on a mission to rescue Gibbs. He sails into Buccaneer Bay, hoping to go unnoticed.

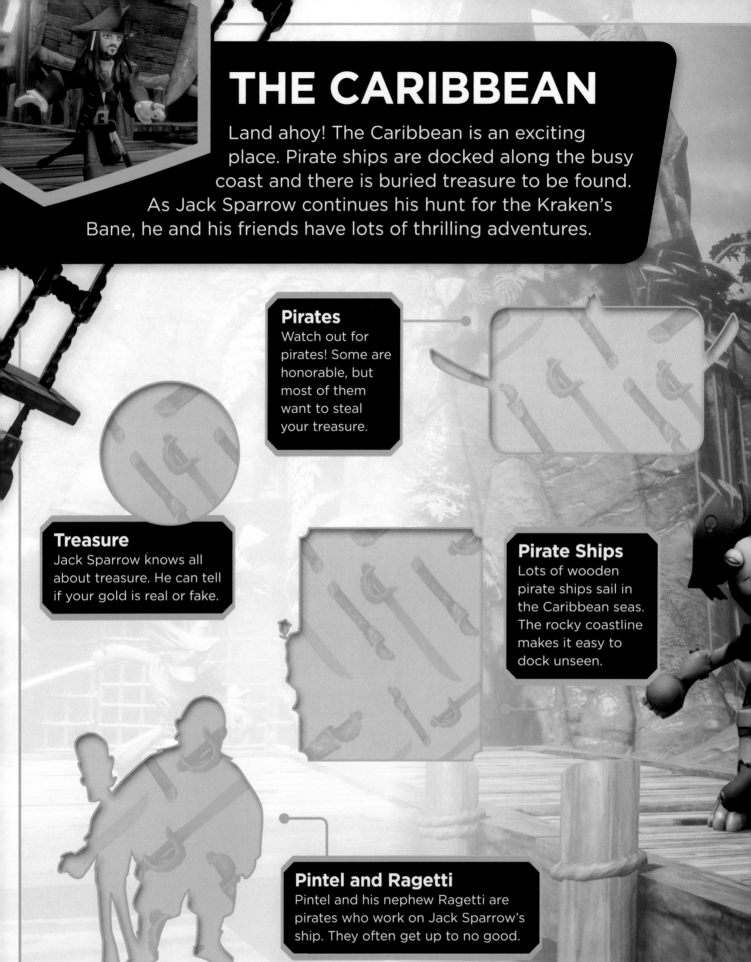

THE CARIBBEAN

Land ahoy! The Caribbean is an exciting place. Pirate ships are docked along the busy coast and there is buried treasure to be found. As Jack Sparrow continues his hunt for the Kraken's Bane, he and his friends have lots of thrilling adventures.

Pirates
Watch out for pirates! Some are honorable, but most of them want to steal your treasure.

Treasure
Jack Sparrow knows all about treasure. He can tell if your gold is real or fake.

Pirate Ships
Lots of wooden pirate ships sail in the Caribbean seas. The rocky coastline makes it easy to dock unseen.

Pintel and Ragetti
Pintel and his nephew Ragetti are pirates who work on Jack Sparrow's ship. They often get up to no good.

DEADLY DUEL
Can Barbossa defeat
Turtle and find one of
the missing pieces of
the Kraken's Bane?

TRAVEL IN STYLE

Who wants to walk when when you can fly through the air, speed over hills in a monster carriage, or surf your way into an adventure? Woody, Wreck-It Ralph, and all their friends love borrowing gadgets and vehicles from each other. It is amazing how many different ways there are to get around!

Anna with Wings!
Princess Anna has found an exciting new way to get to and from her castle—she wears a pair of Condor wings.

Surfing with Stitch
Stitch hasn't always loved surfing—until he learned to use his surfboard to soar through the skies!

It's a Race!
Sulley wears Buzz Lightyear's jetpack, Jack Skellington has Mr. Incredible's hover board, and Ralph rides on Dumbo. Who will win the race?

Captain Hook's Ship
For large groups of people, this roomy flying ship is perfect for traveling in style.

WOODY'S NEW TOY
Woody is used to traveling on his horse Bullseye, but he borrows Buzz's jetpack when he's in a rush.

Monster Wheels
Jack Sparrow is surprised when the dainty carriage he borrowed from Cinderella sprouts huge monster wheels!

Beep Beep!
Vanellope von Schweetz drives Mickey's bright red jalopy. She loves beeping the horn!

Cruella's Car
If Cruella de Vil's not looking, you can borrow her car! It's very comfortable, but will it turn you evil?

ANDY'S TOYS

Andy's toys are heading out into deep space. Buzz Lightyear knows all about space travel, so he will have to help his friends out. There are many exciting challenges to be faced in space, including zero gravity, aliens, and piloting a spaceship!

Woody
Woody is a cowboy. He is not used to space travel. But he is brave and clever—he can't wait to blast off into space!

ALIEN PLANET
When the toys touch down on an alien planet, Jessie can't wait to explore!

Buzz Lightyear
Space Ranger Buzz is excited to return to space. He has missed it!

Jessie
Cowgirl Jessie used to be scared of the dark. But she is not afraid of space as it is full of bright stars.

Hamm and Rex
Hamm and Rex are ready for adventure. Rex hopes he will be scary enough!

Working Together
Sometimes Woody and Buzz disagree, but they always work it out in the end.

Astro Hovercraft
Buzz has a super-fast hover machine that's perfect for outer space adventures.

Bullseye
Woody's horse Bullseye never thought he'd journey into space. But Jessie is helping him learn to gallop in zero gravity!

Slinky
Little Slinky is a loyal friend to Woody. When Woody becomes a Space Ranger, Slinky becomes a Space Dog!

SPACE STORIES

Woody, Jessie, Buzz, and their friends have become brave Space Rangers. When their old alien pals are in trouble, the team blast-off to the rescue! There are many dangers on the alien planet, including goo-blasting volcanoes and the terrifying Emperor Zurg. Can the Space Rangers save the day?

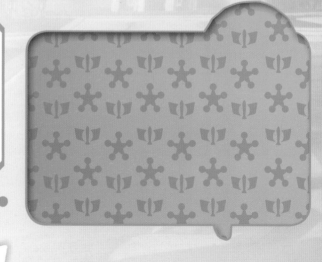

Space Rangers
Buzz and Rex are ready to help their alien friends—if they can find them...

Alien Treasure
Woody helps the aliens unearth gold and crystals buried in the ground.

A Gooey Threat
The alien city is built next to a goo volcano. The goo is precious, but an explosion would be dangerous.

Goo Eruption
Oh no! The volcano is erupting! Buzz and Jessie charge to the rescue. Will they avoid getting buried in goo?

Zurg
The evil Emperor Zurg is out to conquer the alien city. Can the Space Rangers stop him in time?

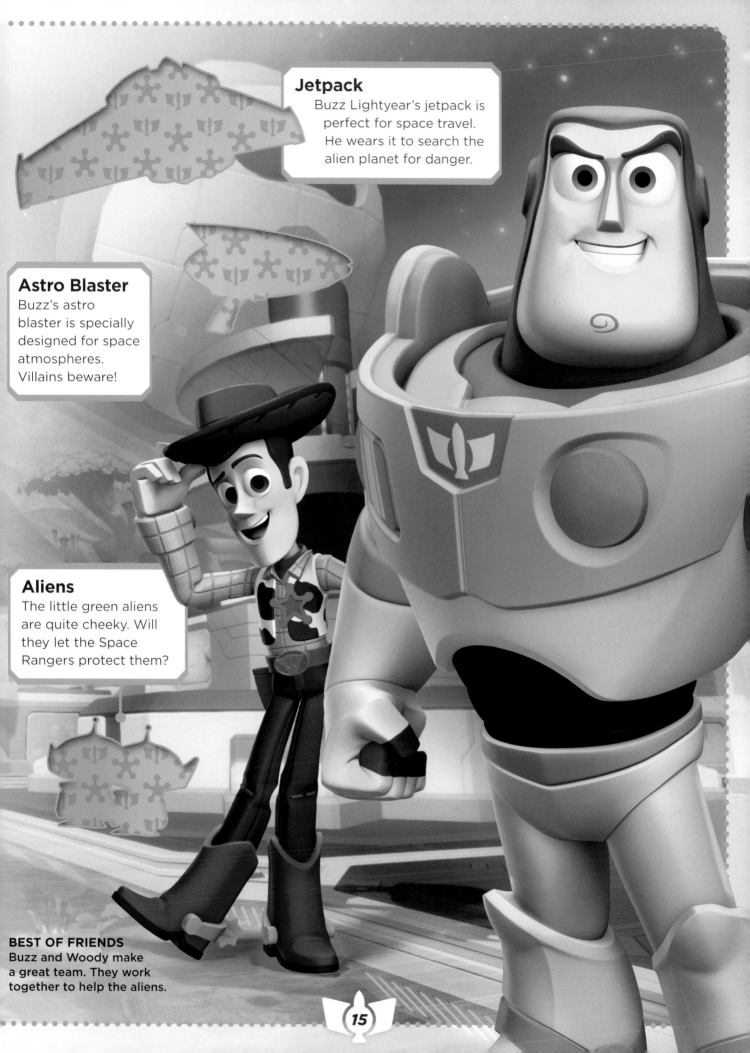

Jetpack
Buzz Lightyear's jetpack is perfect for space travel. He wears it to search the alien planet for danger.

Astro Blaster
Buzz's astro blaster is specially designed for space atmospheres. Villains beware!

Aliens
The little green aliens are quite cheeky. Will they let the Space Rangers protect them?

BEST OF FRIENDS
Buzz and Woody make a great team. They work together to help the aliens.

15

READY TO RACE!

The racecars of Radiator Springs are excited. Luigi has been accepted to take part in an International Race Invitational! His good friends join forces to help with his training. But as the race draws closer, Luigi begins to worry about his racing rivals. Will he be able to overcome the challenges of racing and speed into first place?

Lightning McQueen
Lightning is one of the world's best racecars! He is very excited to prepare Luigi for the race.

Luigi
Luigi loves racing. He was part of Team Lightning during the World Grand Prix. Now he can't wait to get on the racetrack himself!

Casa Della Tires
Luigi is an expert on tires. He just adores them! He even owns his own tire shop, Casa Della Tires.

Mater
Mater is Lightning's best friend. He is the only tow truck in town —and is proud of it!

Holley and Finn

As Luigi prepares for the big race, his British friends, Holley Shiftwell and Finn McMissile, arrive to help.

Racing Rivalry

Francesco Bernoulli is one of Lightning's biggest rivals. Now the Italian racer plans to race against Luigi.

Training

Holley is a spy, so she knows all about weapons. She teaches Lightning and his friends some new racing tricks.

Guido

Guido is Luigi's best friend. He will help change Luigi's tires during the race—and cheer him on, of course!

HAPPY TO HELP
Lightning is going to teach Luigi all the racing skills he has learned during his career.

RADIATOR SPRINGS

It used to be a quiet, dusty town, but Radiator Springs is now a busy tourist hotspot! As the cars prepare for an International Race Invitational, famous racecars from around the world arrive in town. The local cars are geared up for an exciting race—and lots of fun!

Main Street
Main Street runs right through Radiator Springs. Lightning and his pals zoom along it at top speeds!

Tow Mater
As the owner of Tow Mater Towing and Salvage, Mater proudly helps out any cars who have broken down.

Chick Hicks
Chick Hicks is in town for one reason only—to win the race! He hates coming in second, so he will do whatever it takes to win.

ITALIAN RACER
Francesco Bernoulli is one of the world-famous racers to arrive in Radiator Springs.

Cozy Cone Motel
The international racecars are all staying at the Cozy Cone Motel. They have decorated their rooms with their country's flags.

USE YOUR EXTRA STICKERS TO CREATE YOUR OWN SCENE.

NEW FRIENDS

Some people are big, some are small. Some love battling evil, while others would rather play pranks. But that doesn't mean they can't be friends! Buzz Lightyear loves playing hide-and-go-seek, while some of his new friends prefer racing, flying, and crime-fighting. There are so many adventures to choose from!

Rescue Mission
Anna is on a mission to find her missing sister, Elsa. Jessie is excited to help!

On Guard!
In a friendly duel, will Phineas and his pink flamingo mallet defeat the expert swordsman Jack Sparrow?

Elephant Riders
Mike and Woody share a love of elephants. Dumbo and Abu are a great way to get around!

HIDING HORSE
Buzz is looking for Bullseye, the horse. Where could he be?

On Your Bikes!
Syndrome wants a day off from evil—so he joins Buzz and Woody for an energetic bike ride!

Search Party
Jessie's old pal Woody has gone missing! Luckily, her new friends Sulley and Jack Sparrow set out to find him.

Top Team
A princess and a skeleton might seem like a strange team. But together, Rapunzel and Jack Skellington are on the hunt for deadly villains.

On Your Marks...
It's racing time! Who has the fastest steed? Mrs. Incredible, the Lone Ranger, Mike, or Tonto?

Double Trouble
When Wreck-It Ralph teams up with platypus spy Agent P, there is no villain they can't defeat.

THE LONE RANGER

John Reid is the Lone Ranger—a masked horseman who protects the people of the Wild West from danger. When John's town, Colby, is attacked by a gang of ruthless cowboys, he and his crime-fighting partner, Tonto, vow to capture the villains before they take control of the entire West.

Lone Ranger
John Reid wears a black mask to keep his identity as the Lone Ranger a secret.

Tonto
Tonto is a Comanche Indian warrior. He wears warpaint on his face and a dead crow on his head.

Scout
Tonto is a skillful horse rider. His brown and white horse is called Scout.

Town in Trouble
Colby is a small town. Reid wants to keep it safe from traveling thugs.

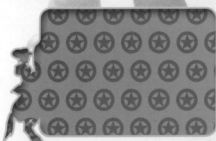

On Target
Reid is a top marksman. He can hit his target from almost any distance.

HI HO SILVER
Reid's trusty mount is
called Silver. He is the
fastest horse in the West.

USE YOUR EXTRA
STICKERS TO CREATE
YOUR OWN SCENE.

THE WILD WEST

The Wild West is a lawless place. Fast trains thunder from town to town, bringing crime and corruption with them. Gold and silver mines are plundered for their riches. When Butch Cavendish and his gang of thugs attack the small town of Colby, it is up to John Reid—the Lone Ranger—and Tonto to stop them.

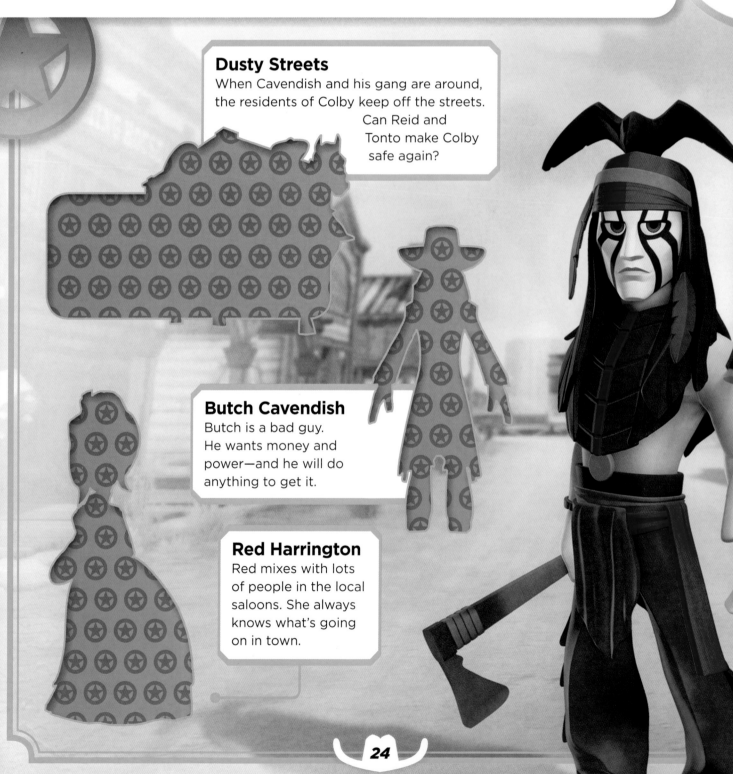

Dusty Streets
When Cavendish and his gang are around, the residents of Colby keep off the streets. Can Reid and Tonto make Colby safe again?

Butch Cavendish
Butch is a bad guy. He wants money and power—and he will do anything to get it.

Red Harrington
Red mixes with lots of people in the local saloons. She always knows what's going on in town.

Fast Trains

Whoever owns the railways has a lot of power. Trains are the quickest way to travel, but are they safe?

LAW AND ORDER
The Lone Ranger and Tonto won't give up until justice has been served.

Cowboy Gang

Butch's gang of cowboys ride through the town, stealing and destroying whatever crosses their paths.

Crime Fighters

John Reid and Tonto are the only pair brave enough to confront Butch and his gang. Look out Butch!

TNT

TNT is a powerful explosive. Reid and Tonto use it to demolish the train tracks, stopping Butch and his gang.

THE INCREDIBLES

The Incredibles are not exactly an ordinary family. They are a family of superheroes! Each of them has an amazing superpower, which they try to hide so they can live a normal life. But when evil strikes, the Incredibles put on their masks and race to the rescue.

Dash
Dash might be young, but he is fearless! He uses his super speed to run rings around villains.

No Ordinary Family
Mr. and Mrs. Incredible try to live a quiet life, but it is difficult to hide their superpowers from the world.

Violet
Violet can create force fields and turn invisible. Her super suit turns invisible with her, too!

Incredicar
In his super-speedy car, Mr. Incredible can find the source of danger in no time. The car can also fire deadly energy bolts.

26

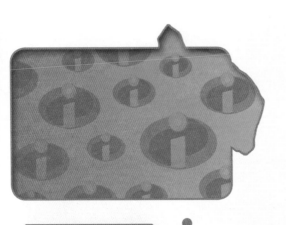

Incredicopter
Dash loves flying the Incredicopter through the skies, searching for anyone causing trouble.

Mr. Incredible
Mr. Incredible is the strongest man in the world. He uses his immense strength to help people in danger.

Mrs. Incredible
Mrs. Incredible can twist and stretch her body like elastic. She uses her stretching abilities to fight crime.

Glide Pack
When Mr. Incredible wears his glide pack, he can soar above skyscrapers and attack his enemies from the air!

Hover Board
The hover board allows the heroes to "surf" through the city. The villains won't even see them coming!

METROVILLE

The city of Metroville is in danger! Insane villain Syndrome and his Omnidroids are trying to destroy the city. The Incredibles come to the rescue, but they don't realize that Syndrome has a secret plan...

Flying Villain
Dash has found Syndrome at the city docks. The genius villain has a suit that allows him to fly.

City People
The residents of Metroville are scared. Will the Incredibles save them?

Syndrome
Syndrome looks like a supervillain—but he doesn't have any powers. Instead, he uses a weapon called zero-point energy.

City Defender
Mr. Incredible is proud of his beautiful city. He won't let Syndrome destroy it!

Omnidroid Army

Syndrome unleashes an army of deadly Omnidroid robots. They are programmed to scan and save the Incredibles' powers.

Mirage

Mirage helps Syndrome with his wicked plan, but she soon realizes how evil he is. So she tries to make amends.

Arch Enemy

Syndrome's real name is Buddy Pine. He used to be a huge fan of Mr. Incredible. Now, he hates all superpowered people.

WATCH OUT!
Syndrome is an evil genius. When he is on the attack, beware!

Edna Mode

Edna designed all of the Incredibles' costumes and gadgets. The Incredibles need her now more than ever!

Force Field

Violet creates a powerful force field to defeat the Omnidroids. But the Omnidroids are secretly scanning her powers.

CRAZY ADVENTURES

Adventures can happen anywhere: in princess castles, on rooftops, even on a rocky cliff. Wreck-It Ralph likes to jump through fiery hoops, while Lightning McQueen wants to race, race, race. Davy Jones plans to steal more treasure, but Jack Sparrow wants to take a break from pirate life. Who wants to go on an adventure?

Flying Friends
Mr. Incredible, Jack Sparrow, and Sulley take to the skies as they explore their new world together.

It's Time for Fun!
Vanellope von Schweetz and Mickey Mouse might be small, but they have BIG ideas for an adventure!

Candy Cart
Vanellope drives her crazy Candy Cart into the middle of a serious race. She jumps straight to the lead!

Who is Faster?
It's the race of the century, starring Lightning McQueen and Dash Incredible. Ready, set, go!

Rooftop Chase
Zurg's evil robots and the Cursed Crew have invaded Monsters University! Will Jessie, Mike, and Mrs. Incredible fight them off?

Clock Tower Siege
Mike and Agent P are determined to stop Davy Jones from stealing the clock tower treasure.

Sliding Around
What a slippery way to travel! Jack Skellington and Violet Incredible try to keep their balance on the pipe slide.

Freezing
Elsa uses her freezing powers to create snow. Now everyone can have a snowball fight!

WRECK IT!
Wreck-It Ralph is training for the annual Super Obstacle Race.

31

GADGETS GALORE

Gadgets are always useful. They add excitement when playing games, they can help defeat evil villains, or they can make your life a little bit easier. From blasters and bats to canes and trains, just grab a gadget and head out on an adventure. What other uses can you think of for these gadgets?

Flamingo Croquet Mallet

A flamingo mallet might not be the best way to hit a ball, but he's very nice to talk to!

Stitch's Blaster

There's nothing better than squirting your foes with green goo! Stitch's blaster has the best goo around.

Carl Fredricksen's Cane

This is the perfect cane. It helps you walk—and it's perfect for hitting things out of your way.

WALL•E's Fire Extinguisher

If there's a fire on your spaceship or an explosion on your train, this handy fire extinguisher will save the day.

BEWARE!
Mr. Incredible is chasing his friends with his new toy—a toilet paper launcher!

WALL·E's Fire Extinguisher

Luigi

Red Zurgbot

Friendly Dinosaur

Freezing

Treasure Hunt

Pizza Planet Truck

Woody

Hamm and Rex

Flying Friends

Don Carlton

Art

Alien Girl

Carl Fredricksen's Cane

Mrs. Incredible

Who is Faster?

Violet

Omnidroid
on the Loose!

Pumpkins at the Ready!

Buzz Lightyear

Tonto

Evil Robot

Tia Dalma

Lightning McQueen

Yellow Monster

Sulley

Cowboy

© Disney. © Disney/Pixar.

Black Ship

It's Time for Fun!

Clam

© Disney. © Disney/Pixar.

Astro Hovercraft

© Disney Enterprises, Inc. and Jerry Bruckheimer, Inc. LONE RANGER ™ & © Classic Media

On Target

© Disney. © Disney/Pixar.

Buzz Flies!

Guido

Vanellope von Schweetz

Bullseye

© Disney. © Disney/Pixar.

Incredicar

Captain Jack Sparrow

© Disney. © Disney/Pixar.

School of Scaring

© Disney. © Disney/Pixar.

Backpack

Dash

Holley and Finn

Wrecking Everything!

Lanterns

Mike's Bike

Mike's Car

Power Steering

Rooftop Chase

Sliding Around

Jessie Finds a Cat

Ralph

Lone Ranger

Casa Della Tires

Randy

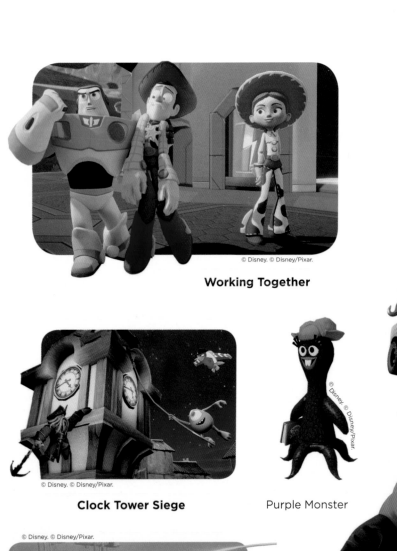

Working Together

Buccaneer Bay

Clock Tower Siege

Purple Monster

A Car's Best Friend

Scrooge

No Ordinary
Family

Glide Pack

Wall•E

Medical Ball

Racing Cup

Squishy

Chernabog

Buzz and Bullseye

Candy Cart

Slinky

Jack Skellington's World

Incredicopter

Hector Barbossa

Damageinator

Look Out!

Town in Trouble

Davy Jones

Nightmare

Green Monster

Alice

To Infinity and Beyond!

Merlin

Monster Bike

Elsa Drives Fast!

Racing Rivalry

Training

Bolt

Flamingo
Croquet
Mallet

Hover Board

Stitch's Blaster

Unlikely Friends

Cursed Crew

Mr. Incredible

Scout

Goo Zurgbot

Alien Tourist

Mulan's
Firework
Cannon

Condor Man
Wings

Mater

Gibbs

Jessie

Scare Team

City People

Silver

Zurg

Goo Blaster

Speeding Train

Tow Mater

On Your Bikes!

Wrecking It!

Zurg's Wrath

Chick Hicks

Pirate Ships

Sheriff

Beep Beep!

Dusty Streets

Search Party

Cutlass

Syndrome

Zurg's Blaster

Rescue Mission

Red Harrington

Incredible Glider

Dumbo Ride

Star Ball

Highway Sign

Practice Makes Perfect

Violet's Power

Anna with Wings!

Flying Villain

Star Command

Goo Eruption

Living in Fear

Anna

Pirates

Splash Pool

Incredible Rescue!

Cruella's Car

Ready for Fun!

Jetpack

Fear Tech Monsters

Vanellope

Alien Treasure

Butch Cavendish

Captain Hook's Ship

Cowboy Gang

Finn McMissile

Terri and Terry

Hamm

Give 'Em a Hand

Attack Chopper

Monster Candy

TNT

Omnidroid Army

On Guard!

Aliens

Double Trouble

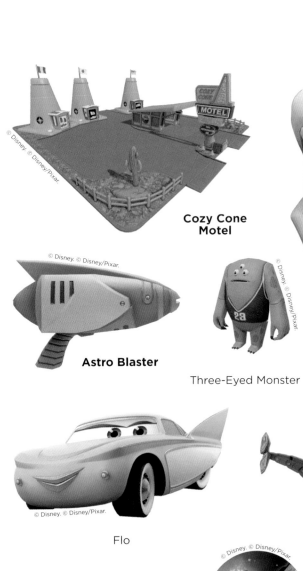

Cozy Cone Motel

Astro Blaster

Three-Eyed Monster

Mirage

Flo

Omnidroid

It's a Race!

Sulley's Race

Sorcerer's Apprentice Mickey

Treasure Chest

Soccer ball

Arch Enemy

No Place is Safe

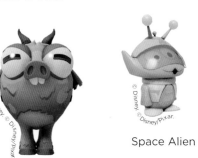

Archie the Scare Pig

Space Alien

Pintel and Ragetti

Edna Mode

Main Street

Belle

Monster Wheels

Mike and Bullseye

Space Rangers

Agent P

Fix-it Felix

Fillmore

Elephant Riders

On Your Marks...

Sweet Ride

Treasure

City Defender

Phone It In Launcher

Fast Trains

© Disney Enterprises, Inc. and Jerry Bruckheimer, Inc. LONE RANGER TM & © Classic Media

A Gooey Threat

© Disney. © Disney/Pixar.

Toilet Paper Launcher

© Disney. © Disney/Pixar.

Crime Fighters

© Disney Enterprises, Inc. and Jerry Bruckheimer, Inc. LONE RANGER TM & © Classic Media

Ramone

© Disney/Pixar. Chevrolet Impala™
© Disney.

Rapunzel

© Disney. © Disney/Pixar.

Captain Jack's Ship

© Disney. © Disney/Pixar.

Go Fish Launcher

© Disney. © Disney/Pixar.

Surfing with Stitch

© Disney. © Disney/Pixar.

Rex

© Disney. © Disney/Pixar.

Mike's Fireworks

© Disney. © Disney/Pixar.

Top Team

© Disney. © Disney/Pixar.

Caribbean House

© Disney. © Disney/Pixar.

Force Field

© Disney. © Disney/Pixar.

EXTRA STICKERS

EXTRA STICKERS

© Disney. © Disney/Pixar.

© Disney. © Disney/Pixar.

© Disney. © Disney/Pixar.

© Disney. © Disney/Pixar.

© Disney. © Disney/Pixar.

© Disney. © Disney/Pixar.

© Disney. © Disney/Pixar.

© Disney. © Disney/Pixar.

© Disney. © Disney/Pixar.

© Disney Enterprises, Inc. and Jerry Bruckheimer, Inc. LONE RANGER TM & © Classic Media

© Disney Enterprises, Inc. and Jerry Bruckheimer, Inc. LONE RANGER TM & © Classic Media

EXTRA STICKERS

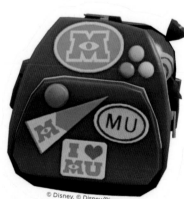

EXTRA STICKERS

EXTRA STICKERS

© Disney. © Disney/Pixar.
© Disney. © Disney/Pixar.
© Disney. © Disney/Pixar.
© Disney. © Disney/Pixar.
© Disney. © Disney/Pixar.
© Disney. © Disney/Pixar.
© Disney/Pixar.
© Disney. © Disney/Pixar.
© Disney. © Disney/Pixar.
© Disney. © Disney/Pixar.
© Disney. © Disney/Pixar.
© Disney. © Disney/Pixar.

EXTRA STICKERS

EXTRA STICKERS

EXTRA STICKERS

TOW MATER

EXTRA STICKERS

EXTRA STICKERS

© Disney. © Disney/Pixar.

EXTRA STICKERS

EXTRA STICKERS

EXTRA STICKERS

EXTRA STICKERS

© Disney Enterprises, Inc. and Jerry Bruckheimer, Inc. LONE RANGER TM & © Classic Media

© Disney. © Disney/Pixar.

© Disney Enterprises, Inc. and Jerry Bruckheimer, Inc. LONE RANGER TM & © Classic Media

© Disney. © Disney/Pixar. Chevrolet Impala™

© Disney. © Disney/Pixar.

© Disney. © Disney/Pixar.

© Disney. © Disney/Pixar.

© Disney. © Disney/Pixar.

© Disney. © Disney/Pixar.

© Disney

© Disney/Pixar.

© Disney. © Disney/Pixar.

© Disney. © Disney/Pixar.

© Disney. © Disney/Pixar.

EXTRA STICKERS

EXTRA STICKERS